# Malvina House Hotel
# Its artwork and its history

Contact us:
stonerunstudio.net
malvinahousehotel.com
sealedpr.com


Published by Stanley Services Publications

Printed at The Orcadian, Hell's Half Acre, Hatston, Kirkwall,
Orkney, KW15 1DW - www.orcadian.co.uk

Researched, written and designed by SeAled PR Ltd. for Stanley Services
Ltd., Stanley, Falkland Islands.

# Malvina House Hotel
# Its artwork and its history

The house, the hotel and the landscapes of
Falkland Islands artist Richard Cockwell.

By Lisa Watson, SeAled PR
For Stanley Services Ltd.

Bibliography and acknowledgements

Wrecks of the Falkland Islands by John Smith
A visitor's guide to the Falkland Islands by Debbie Summers
The Dictionary of Falklands Biography edited by David Tatham
South American Missionary Society By Rev. Peter J. Millam
Old Falkland Photos compiled by Shane Wolsey
Atmosphere, Landscapes of the Falkland Islands by Ian and Georgina Strange
New Island Falkland Islands. A South Atlantic Wildlife Sanctuary for Conservation Management
Place names of the Falkland Islands edited by Richard Munro
falklands.info
naval-history.net
mainpointfarm.co.uk
liverpoolmuseums.org.uk
falklandswildlife.com


With particular thanks to Mrs Joan Spruce for her wonderful notes and thank you also to the Falkland Islands Government Planning Office, the Falkland Islands Government Philatelic Bureau, Mr Peter Pepper, Mr Terry Spruce, Mr Nicholas Pitaluga, Mr Ron Binnie, Mr Neil Watson, Mr Tex Alazia, Mr Ian Strange, Miss Teryn Joshua, Mr Tony Chater and Mrs Bunny Bonner for so much useful information. Thanks also to the proof readers Mr John Fowler, Mr Mike Rendell, Mrs Jackie Summers, Mrs Jenny Cockwell and Mr Nigel Knight.


ISBN 978-0-9566756-0-6

# CONTENTS

Page 4: Malvina today: Includes images of Malvina Manager Carl Stroud and Head Chef Matt Clark.
Page 6: Clockwise from left - the original Malvina House hall, JJ with wife Sara and son, the original Malvina House drawing room, the original Malvina House, Malvina Felton. Images courtesy of the Falkland Islands Museum and National Trust.
Page 8: Images of the artist Richard Cockwell at his house on Ross Road West, Stanley. Photographs by Lisa Watson, SeAled PR.

All paintings and sketches by Richard Cockwell.
Paintings photographed by Brian Jamieson, South Harbour Consulting.

Book design by Sarah Clement and Lisa Watson, SeAled PR.

I am delighted to introduce this book which is a culmination of a great deal of effort by a number of people.

In 2004 Stanley Services Limited agreed to purchase the Malvina House Hotel which had been ably owned and operated by Mr Mike Rendell since the 1980's. We were determined to build on the excellent work undertaken by Mike and have subsequently invested substantially to make it the Falkland Islands premier hotel. As part of this investment the Company recognised the need to increase the number of bedrooms from 17 to 36 – these were completed in January 2010. During the design of these rooms we wanted them to be modern, comfortable, light and environmentally friendly but with a "Falklands Flavour" to remind all our guests that they are in a very special location of the world.

I have had the fortune to know Richard Cockwell since 1987 and a few years ago we were both sitting in a meeting and I noticed that he had drawn a very elaborate 'doodle'. After the meeting we discussed his love of painting and I asked him to paint for me what I think is one of the most iconic landmarks on the Islands - the Cape Pembroke Lighthouse. Richard, in his usual modest manner, doubted that I would like it; needless to say it was a fantastic painting and I am very proud of it.

Richard also painted some landscapes which hang in our bar and lounge. When we were discussing the new extension Richard came up with the idea that each room should be named after a Falklands location and he would paint the relevant landscapes. This involved a great deal of work, effort and skill by Richard but as I am sure you will agree he has produced exquisite paintings which give exactly the Falklands flavour that we were seeking for our new bedrooms. We also hope that you find SeAled PR's brief history of the important sites reflected in Richard's art helpful.

I was very fortunate to see all the paintings prior to them being hung in each of the new rooms and I thought it would be a good idea if they could be shown all together in a book so that people from all over the world could enjoy Richard's creative paintings of the Falkland Islands.

I hope you will enjoy this book.

Tom Swales
Managing Director
Stanley Services Limited

The original Malvina House, on the site of which the present hotel now sits, has a history that stretches back to the fascinating early days of Stanley.

In 1849 an 8-year-old John James Felton and his family made the long journey to the Falkland Islands on board merchant ship *Victory*. His father was one of a number of military pensioners offered the opportunity to settle in the Falkland Islands.

As a young man John James, or JJ as he was known, threw himself into establishing a sheep farm on East Falklands, later naming it Evelyn Station after his eldest daughter.

JJ married Sara Turner and the Feltons had seven children, two boys and five girls including Malvina Nathalia born in 1881.

By the 1880's JJ was wealthy enough to build an impressive town house. The resulting 'Malvina House' with its fine conservatory, two large chimneys, balcony, lawn and gardens was named after daughter Malvina.

In David Tatham's 'Dictionary of Falklands Biography', Joan Spruce writes, 'This house was to be the social hub for many naval visitors, and other young men who were attracted to the vivacious daughters.'

In particular the young people were fond of organizing pantomimes and photographs from the time, show jolly groups of women, men and children dressed as fairy queens, dames and pageboys.

JJs obituary in the *Falkland Islands Magazine & Church Paper* of 1911 described him as a tall figure 'to be seen daily working at his house and garden in which he took so much pride.'

Malvina Felton later became the wife of Admiral Lawson.

In 1930 the house was purchased by William Luxton and in 1967 was demolished, apart from the conservatories, and rebuilt.

William Luxton's granddaughters Sally Blake and Judy Summers sold the house to Don and Margaret Davidson who opened it as a guesthouse, and in 1983 it was sold on to Mike and Phyllis Rendell who completed the transformation of the house into a comfortable hotel with modern facilities.

Stanley Services Ltd. who purchased the hotel in 2004, have since refurbished, and most recently, added twenty rooms.

Richard Cockwell was born in England in 1939 and raised in Hampshire and Wiltshire within an agricultural setting.

He was educated at Stanbridge Earls School in Hampshire

In 1964 he was employed by Packe Brothers and Company Limited of Fox Bay East, Falkland Islands, as Assistant Manager of their 150,000 acre sheep farm. Richard became Manager of the farm in 1967 and was living there during the Falklands Conflict of 1982.

In 1985 Richard built and opened the Falkland Mill designed to process Falklands' wool into yarn and knitwear. Although the mill produced an attractive product it closed due to the high cost of energy and labour.

In 1997 after a brief period of running a road building project sponsored by the Government, as well as developing a graphic design business in Fox Bay, he was elected as a Member of the Legislative Council for the Camp Constituency. After moving to Stanley in 2001 he was elected as a Stanley Councillor.

Richard is now retired but continues to paint. In 2009 he was commissioned by Stanley Services Ltd. to produce a series of watercolour landscapes to hang in the new rooms of Malvina.

Richard notes that having been interested in art in all of its forms since school, "...it seems strange that I did not indulge except for a few sessions of once a week night classes in wood carving (he has a carving of a mother and child in Whiteparish church in Wiltshire) when in my early 20s.

"Having lived in the Falklands for a number of years I was only too aware of the magnificent scenery that I wished to record.

"However, being busy managing a 150,000 acre sheep station and latterly attempting to establish a wool mill, I did nothing further.

"After being elected to the Legislative Council, I was in Britain for meetings and found myself with two weeks free. I decided that I did not want to sit on a beach for that time so - it being my sixtieth birthday - decided to take a painting holiday in the South of France. This holiday course was run by the accomplished artist David McEwen.

"David encouraged me and I became an avid watercolourist."

Situated on the east coast of East Falklands, Stanley Harbour is accessible by sea through a narrow entrance from the larger harbour of Port William. The east head of the 'Narrows' is known as Engineer Point, and the west head Navy Point. Both points are shown to the left and right of the painting.

In 1842 Moody, the Lieutenant Governor of Port Louis, was instructed by Lord Stanley, the British Secretary of State for War and the Colonies, to research the potential of the Port William area as the site for a new capital.

The following year it was concluded that Port William afforded a good deep-water anchorage and the south shore of Port Jackson was a suitable location for the proposed settlement.

Construction began in July 1843, and in 1845 the new capital was officially named after Lord Stanley.

Later that decade Stanley saw a dramatic increase in the number of visiting ships partly due to the California Gold Rush.

The boom in ship provisioning and ship-repair was also aided by the unfortunate effects on ships of the cruel seas around Cape Horn.

Stanley and the Falkland Islands are famous as the repository of many wrecks of nineteenth century ships that reached the islands to be condemned and then often employed as floating warehouses by local merchants.

After a busy period for the port the introduction of iron steamships in the 1890s and the opening of the Panama Canal in 1914 reduced trade drastically.

Stanley continued supporting whaling and sealing activities and later British warships (and garrisons) and later still, the fishing and cruise ship industries.

Stanley was initially populated by colonists from Port Louis (or Anson as it was once briefly referred to) but was further expanded by the arrival of 30 married Chelsea Pensioners and their families. The Chelsea Pensioners were to form the permanent garrison and police force taking over from the Royal Sappers and Miners Regiment who had garrisoned the early colony.

Some of Stanley's earliest buildings include Government House, the colonists' cottages on Pioneer Row and Drury Street and those in the dockyard.

Beached at the Eastern end of Stanley Harbour in Whalebone Cove, the *Lady Elizabeth* was forced to end her days in the Falklands after she struck the Uranie Rock in the entrance to Berkeley Sound north east of Stanley.

She arrived in the islands on March 13, 1913, on a voyage from Vancouver to Delagoa Bay, with a cargo of lumber.

So badly damaged by the Uranie Rock it was decided to dispose of her, and the *Lady Elizabeth* served as a floating warehouse in the harbour for many years until she broke her moorings and became beached in Whalebone Cove in 1936.

The *Lady Elizabeth* had made a number of visits to the Falklands prior to this, on at least one occasion carrying the materials for the construction of Christ Church Cathedral.

Built in 1879 in Sunderland UK, the three masted barque had a registered tonnage of 1,208, a length of 223 ft and a beam of 35ft.

Beached in the late 1930s the remains of the *Plym* are near *Lady Elizabeth* on the north eastern shore of the harbour. Used as a steam tug she was built at Plymouth in 1903 by Messrs. Willoughby Brothers, her length was 50ft and her beam 10ft.

Stanley Harbour itself is unparalleled as a ship graveyard of nineteenth century international shipping. Former Manager of Falkland Islands Tourism, Graham Bound in his 'Maritime History Trail' admits that Stanley was not usually a captain's first choice when facing difficulties, for the port had a bad name among mariners.

While the people of Stanley did not actually stoop to 'wrecking' the unhappy captain might discover that due to the extortionate rates of repairs, it would often make more sense to sell the ship locally as a storage hulk, jetty head or as building materials.

Whalebone Cove was also the site from which flooded ship HMS *Canopus* fired the opening shots in the Battle of the Falklands.

Bound says "It is said that the first ranging shots were so accurate that the vanguard of the German squadron immediately turned away."

The guns were directed from an observation point on a hill to the east; since named Canopus.

Cape Pembroke forms the eastern-most point of the Falkland Islands and the south headland of Port William, within which, on its south side, is Stanley Harbour.

The headland was named after Thomas, Earl of Pembroke and Montgomery.

As an aid to shipping, in 1854 a cast iron lighthouse replaced the wooden navigation marker. In 1855 a lighthouse keeper was appointed and the light illuminated for the first time.

The lighthouse was 60 feet high and painted with red and white bands, the light itself 110 feet tall and visible in good weather for 14 miles.

In a 'Notice to Mariners' published by the Hydrographic Office in London in 1856 it is noted, 'The Colonial Government at the Falkland Islands has given notice that a fixed light of the natural colour was established on Cape Pembroke on the first of December last. ...A vessel entering Port William will leave the light on the port hand; and the Master should be careful to observe that, as the flood tide sets strongly to the northward, and the ebb to the southward in passing Cape Pembroke, he should not pass between this Cape and the Seal Rocks unless the ship is under steam or has a good commanding breeze; in light winds or much swell it is better to pass outside.'

The lighthouse was eventually taken down to its base and a new one built in 1906.

Sadly the lighthouse was badly vandalized in the early 1980s after the Falklands War, and ceased to function. However, in an effort to preserve the handsome structure the Lighthouse Trust replaced the glass prisms and tower glass and funded the refurbishment of the structure.

A modern navigation light is positioned to the South East of the old lighthouse.

Cape Pembroke itself is a popular leisure area for walkers and runners and is included in the Stanley Running Club half marathon route.

Today, a memorial to *Atlantic Conveyer* - A British merchant navy ship, sunk during the Falklands War of 1982 - stands nearby.

A metal plaque showing a panorama of the mountains west of Stanley stands in front of the lighthouse.

The Two Sisters are part of the recognizable backdrop of mountains to the west of Stanley. When viewed from a distance the peaks appear to be the same height and of similar shape, hence the name.

Historically, paintings of the twin peaks are depicted with a degree of grandeur that has much to do with artistic licence.

Richard Cockwell's view is entirely realistic, but unusual in that it shows the western side, painted from a point on Mount Kent Road.

The eastern side of the Two Sisters Mountains overlooks Stanley, the old Two Sisters Road in Moody Valley as well as the site of the old Moody Brook Royal Marine Barracks (destroyed by Argentine forces on April 2,1982.).

Built in the 1930's the Two Sisters Road was intended as the beginning of a road network to the north camp but never completed.

Many years later farmer Dick Hills, who owned the land around the road and Two Sisters Mountains, purchased a stone crusher with business partner Bob Ross. The two cleverly created a small 'rail road' that moved crushed rock in trucks down the valley.

The trucks were hauled up the valley by an old land rover adapted to fit on the rails. The old stone crusher still sits on the edge of the road part of the way up Moody Valley.

Prior to the building of the north camp road system in the 1990's the Two Sisters Road was most often traversed in the 1980's by farmers in land rovers on their journeys to and from newly purchased farms in the north of East Falklands

In recent history, Two Sisters Mountains were one of the main Argentine defences of Stanley during the Falklands War of 1982. It was the task of 45 Commando Royal Marines to battle the Argentine 4th Infantry Regiment during the struggle for peaks on June 11 and 12; two days before the Argentine surrender.

Despite the loss of three Royal Marines and a Sapper of the Royal Engineers, the commandos fought through sniper, heavy machine gun, mortar and artillery fire, and by dawn the peaks were in the hands of the British forces.

Eleven soldiers received gallantry awards.

Falklands folklore tells of a band of gauchos pursuing a troop of wild horses along a mountain top at such great speed that the animals were unable to halt when they came upon a sheer cliff. The horses fell to their deaths, hence the name Mount Tumbledown.

South American gauchos were among the earliest settlers in the Falkland Islands. Their skill as horsemen and stockmen was vital in those challenging days.

Today Falkland Islanders still use some of the old gaucho names to refer to the various parts of their horse tack and to horse colours.

At Port Louis in March 1833 Captain Fitzroy of the *Beagle* wrote: "The gauchos wished to leave the place, and return to the Plata, but as they were the only useful labourers on the islands, in fact, the only people on whom any dependence could be placed for a regular supply of fresh beef, I interested myself as much as possible to induce them to remain, and with partial success, for seven staid out of twelve ..."

Situated approximately four miles to the West of Stanley the mountain and surrounding area was primarily utilised as grazing for sheep. Although now owned by the Falkland Islands Government it was once leased to farmer Richard 'Dick' Hills.

Mount Tumbledown became infamous in the Falklands War of 1982 as a result of the bloody battle for the mountain.

During the last days of the War eight men of 2 Scots Guards and one Royal Engineer lost their lives in the ferocious battle while others were wounded in Argentine-laid minefields during the approach.

The British soldiers fought what was thought to be one of the best Argentine units in the Falklands, the 5th Marine Infantry Battalion, and battled under mortar and artillery bombardment with most of the eight dying as a result of sniper fire.

Ultimately the Argentine positions were taken as a result of hand-to-hand fighting with grenades and bayonets. Eleven British soldiers received gallantry awards for their part in the battle.

Tumbledown is still scattered with military paraphernalia from that time including a large Argentine field kitchen.

Mount Longdon, situated to the West of Stanley is most likely to have been named for Sir James Robert Longden, Clerk to the Falkland Islands Governor and afterwards Acting Colonial Secretary and Justice of the Peace.

Longden arrived in the Falkland Islands in 1844, leaving again in 1862.

Up until 1982 Mount Longdon's history was modest but invaluable. Compared to other grazing camps immediately north, the mountain, and its surrounding land offered good quality grass for sheep bred for wool.

In the Falklands today 1,140,500 hectares of similar farmland supports around 600,000 sheep. Mount Longdon is now owned by the Falkland Islands Government and leased by the Watsons of Long Island farm in order to graze around 500 young sheep.

While the grand and sweeping plain in the painting is an accurate depiction of the Longdon landscape, and the white grass a nutritious snack for stock, in 1982 the reality of the terrain for the marching soldier was rather more cruel.

A soldier involved in the advance towards the mountain, a key position overlooking Stanley, wrote of the "...great rivers of rock – big white boulders – and you have to cross them and then there's the heather and the gorse and its constantly wet."

In the battle for Longdon eighteen soldiers of the 3rd Battalion the Parachute Regiment and an attached Royal Engineer were killed, with many more wounded. Three more paratroopers and a Royal Electrical and Mechanical Engineer craftsman were killed in the subsequent shelling.

The British troops fought the Argentine 7th Infantry Regiment, who were initially alerted to the advance of the paratroopers when a soldier of 3 Para stepped on a mine.

In a valiant act at the western end of the mountain, Sergeant Ian McKay collected together a group of his men and moved in to knock out a heavy machine gun post that had pinned down two platoons.

The action led to the posthumous award of the Victoria Cross to Sergeant McKay; he and one of the men were killed, but the enemy position was silenced.

Captain Robert Fitzroy, a hydrographer and surveyor, named Mount William for William, Duke of Clarence, during a visit to the Falklands on his ship *Beagle* in 1833.

On the journey Fitzroy carried with him a young Charles Darwin, and the painting only too accurately illustrates Darwin's impression of the islands, "... the land is low and undulating with stony peaks and bare ridges; it is universally covered by a brown wiry grass, which grows on the peat"

Perhaps not entirely enamoured by the vast space and big skies he added, "The whole landscape ...has an air of extreme desolation ...This is one of the quietest places we have ever been to."

In geological terms the quartzite rocky outcrops that crown Mt William are typical of the Falklands landscape.

The tops of the hills are likely to have been exposed to most of the effects of freezing and thawing caused during the ice age erosion that occurred in the Pleistocene glaciation between 25,000 to 15,000 years ago.

In the early days of Stanley, Mount William was primarily utilised as a grazing area for cattle intended for consumption by the residents of Stanley.

In order to restrict the roaming cattle, several turf walls were built. Some of these can still be seen today, although they are mainly flattened and covered with stumped vegetation.

In later years sheep were grazed on the land and it was more usual to ride out on horseback and bring in cattle for beef from more nutritious pastures further away from Stanley.

Situated south of Tumbledown, Mount William was another important Argentine defensive position due to its situation overlooking Stanley.

On June 13, 1982, one day before the surrender of all Argentine troops in the Falklands the Gurkhas prepared to make a daylight attack on Mount William. Possibly to the disappointment of the fierce little Nepalese warriors, the Argentine troops removed themselves from the slopes and retreated into Stanley. On the morning of June 14 the Gurkhas moved onto the summit without any opposition.

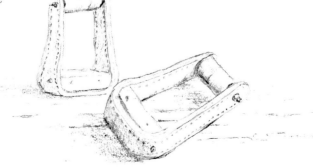

PL
TERSON'S POINT BRIDGE
(FITZROY)
-04-09

The bridge and the settlement of Fitzroy, both situated west of Stanley, are named for ships commander, and surveyor Robert Fitzroy (1805–1865) captain of *Beagle*, during survey voyages to the Falklands.

Built in 1934 the bridge was financed by the Falkland Islands Company with assistance from the Islands' government. The bridge is 12ft wide and over 600ft long and was built primarily to cater for the movement of sheep.

Originally linking land leased by the Yonge family on the north side of Fitzroy River, to Fitzroy Farm on the south side, the bridge greatly shortened the journey between Stanley and Fitzroy and on to Darwin, enabling travellers to avoid the soft countryside north of Mount Pleasant, where the old horse track ran. It also reduced the distance for the annual movement of flocks of sheep for shearing, from Green Patch in the north of East Falklands to Fitzroy and back.

The erection of the wooden bridge which is supported on reinforced concrete piles, began on August 1, 1934 with a gang of fourteen men and was completed by the end of the year.

The Falkland Islands Company's mason, E S Crawford supervised construction. Originally it had been planned that the hulk of the SS *Great Britain* that was beached in Sparrow Cove would be towed to Fitzroy River and sunk as a support for the bridge at the deepest part of the crossing.

It was eventually decided that this would prove too difficult, but the *Great Britain* still made a contribution, as her pitch pine cargo battens were found to be in as good condition as ever, and were put to use as railings for the new bridge.

An image of the Fitzroy River Bridge is also captured on a Falklands 43p stamp from the year 2000, based on a painting by Falklands' artist Mike Peake.

In Richard Cockwell's painting, the misty view behind the bridge includes Mount Challenger.

The mountain sits near the end of an impressive mountain range that runs all the way across East Falklands from Falkland Sound to Stanley. The highest of these is Mount Usborne at 2,312 ft.

Tucked into the south shore of Port Salvador on the north coast of East Falklands is Gibraltar Station, also known as Salvador.

In the 1830s Gibraltarian Andrez Pitaluga, established the station; his descendents still farm there today.

Pitaluga came to the Falklands in 1838 and was taken on as a capataz (foreman) of the Port Louis gauchos. Pitaluga was engaged in catching and taming wild horses and slaughtering wild cattle.

It was not until 1869 that he began to acquire small areas of former Crown Grant land in the Salvador Water area and beyond, eventually only retaining two sections, Gibraltar Station and Rincon Grande before his death in 1878.

The two sections have remained in the family ever since.

Farm development aims included an urgent need to reduce the high numbers of wild cattle, while at the same time establishing sheep for wool production.

This required the erection of many miles of fencing as well as burning pasture in order to reduce the over-growth of whitegrass.

Fencing the property has continued throughout the generations but rotational grazing has been the favoured system for over 35 years now.

The early stock would have been of English flock origins, primarily Romney or Cheviot and Dales type; however, the breeds have long since changed through Corriedale and Polwarth types to the Tasmanian Cormo that is now run for fine wool and meat production.

Previously, when running up to 18,000 head of sheep, the station employed as many as 18 people, but today the stock levels hold at approximately 10,500, with most work carried out by two people, and shearing undertaken by contractors.

In early years, all supplies in, and produce out, had to be carried by schooner, and then horseback.

Today, the station is linked by road, and machinery has replaced the horse but a great deal of history is retained in the stone buildings, and gorse walls plus stone and sod corrals.

Three out of four dwellings and a small barn built in stone by Andrez Pitaluga still exist.

Once the haunt of gauchos and cattle farmers the tiny settlement of Darwin overlooks Choiseul Sound, on the east side of East Falkland's central isthmus.

The stretch of water depicted in the painting was named by French Admiral and explorer Antoine Louis de Bougainville after the French Foreign Secretary, the Duc de Choiseul.

Darwin Settlement itself recalls Charles Darwin who made camp there during a horseback expedition in 1833.

The first 'dwelling' at Darwin was a small hut built close to the Boca turf wall in 1852.

While cattle farming was among Darwin's first agricultural industries, sheep farming came to dominate the area.

Over the years the settlement grew substantially developing into a busy community of approximately 200 people, and in 1872 a schoolhouse building was erected and a schoolmaster brought from Scotland. One year later an iron church was shipped from England and built at Darwin.

In 1875 a tallow works was established at Goose Green nearby where sheep carcasses were rendered down and their fat exported to Britain. Sand banks and tides made it difficult to manoeuvre ships in the bay at Darwin, so the majority of houses and the church were moved to the Goose Green site, with its superior berthing.

Darwin was eventually left with just a few houses, the stone corral, galpon (shed) and flagpole.

In 1956 the land owners, the Falkland Islands Company, erected a boarding school half way between Darwin and Goose Green. Many generations of children from the agricultural sector attended the school until it was closed in 1980.

The original Darwin Manager's house was demolished in 1979 and a new one built close by; later to become the guesthouse Darwin Lodge.

In recent history the area is most often remembered for the battle that took place on the hill above Darwin on May 28, 1982.

Colonel H Jones VC of the 2nd Battalion the Parachute Regiment (2 Para) was among 17 men killed by Argentine forces defending Goose Green.

San Carlos Water
18-02-87

Sheltered from the brisk winds of Falkland Sound, San Carlos Water offers access to San Carlos, one of only two larger settlements on the west coast of East Falklands.

Named after a Spanish sloop that visited in 1768 San Carlos Water jabs into the north west of East Falklands. North over the Verde Mountains and on another prong of water sits the sister settlement Port San Carlos.

In March 1829 plans for a penal colony in the Falklands were first mentioned publicly in Buenos Aires and it is believed that San Carlos was the intended site. However, the plans never came to fruition.

An interesting rogue in San Carlos's colourful history was United States citizen Captain Horton Smylie who operated ship wrecking as well as cattle rustling from bases in the area.

Smylie eventually adopted "respectability' and became the American Consul in Stanley.

The farm of San Carlos was originally leased by John Bonner in 1861 and to differentiate between this and Port San Carlos, it was always known as JB or Bonners, while Port San Carlos leased by Keith Cameron was referred to as KC or Camerons.

Both farms were divided and sold in the 1980s as smaller farm units.

Directly opposite San Carlos is the remains of the Ajax Bay mutton refrigeration plant set up in 1953 for the freezing and export of large numbers of carcasses.

It operated for two seasons before closing down partly due to the logistical problem of moving live sheep to the freezing plant.

Ajax Bay served a worthy purpose in the 1982 War when under Surgeon Commander R T Jolly it was set up as a highly effective Field Dressing Station.

San Carlos Water became infamous when the Argentine air force ran repeated bombing raids on the British naval ships anchored there.

The harbour became known as 'Bomb Alley'.

The primary landing beach for the British Forces is situated at San Carlos and to this day is known as 'Blue Beach', after its forces code name.

Visitors to San Carlos can view the graves of British war dead at Blue Beach cemetery.

The first seat of British Government of the Falkland Islands, and with a fascinating and often bloody history, Port Louis is situated on the coast of Berkeley Sound in the north east of East Falklands.

French settlers under the aristocrat and later admiral, Louis-Antoine de Bougainville, founded the settlement and named it Port Louis in 1764. Following a Spanish takeover in 1767, it was renamed Puerto Soledad, but the Spanish abandoned it in 1811. Luis Vernet re-settled it in 1826, and was granted control under the United Provinces of the River Plate in 1828, when he promptly renamed it Puerto Luis.

Vernet used the settlement as a base for sealing and harvesting the wild cattle for skins and beef. However, a United States warship broke up the settlement in December 1831, in response to Vernet's seizure of American seal hunting ships.

In October 1832, the Provinces sent a tiny garrison and another governor, who was killed in a mutiny.

In January 1833 British control was re-established, and the tiny garrison expelled. But the existing settlers were encouraged to remain – and most did.

A young Charles Darwin paid two visits to the settlement on the *Beagle* under Captain Fitzroy.

Those early years were often dangerous and subject to 'gaucho law'. The most notorious murder being that of five of Vernet's senior employees, including Mathew Brisbane, in August 1833, by Antonio Rivero and other disgruntled gauchos, over a pay dispute.

In 1842 Governor Richard Moody arrived at Port Louis and drew up extensive plans for a new town there, but the order then came from London to move the settlement to Port Jackson (later named Stanley).

From around 1841 colonist John Bull Whitington, who, it is recorded, maintained an uneasy relationship with Moody, farmed sheep at Port Louis. Whitington moved to Stanley in 1849.

Two years later Robert and Edward Packe acquired a lease on the land. The Packe brothers eventually maintained vast holdings on East and West Falklands.

in more recent years Port Louis was owned by the Robson family and now the Gilding family.

The picturesque settlement of Port Howard nestles under Mount Maria, on the long narrow inlet that is now the ferry head on West Falklands.

Port Howard was established as a sheep farm in 1866 by brothers James Lovegrove and Henry Waldron, and since then has prospered under the watchful eye of its managers, not least members of the Lee family, whose ancestor, Jacob, was employed by the farm in 1870.

In 1885 a group of farmers established the Falkland Islands Meat Company, and the Second Creek Slaughterhouse was erected near Port Howard settlement for the processing of mutton carcasses for export.

The company closed shortly afterwards as a result of incurring losses but re-emerged in 1891 and continued for four years. Dissatisfied with the prices they were obtaining, the farmers offered no more sheep for export.

After 1895 buildings and houses were moved from Second Creek to the present settlement site where some remain to this day. The foundations of the freezer works can still be seen at Second Creek.

Port Howard's cultivated fields are surrounded by well kept gorse hedges. The fields were used for grazing and hay making, and in latter years to support the farm dairy.

Robin and Rodney Lee purchased the farm in 1986 and it is now jointly owned by Robin's sons as Port Howard Farming Ltd.

During the 1982 Conflict Port Howard residents were forced to share their normally peaceful settlement with 1,000 Argentine soldiers.

Resident 'Bunny' Bonner recalled those dark days: "I remember the morning the helicopter arrived with the first of them, it carried on all day, they set up tents and dug trenches."

As a result of the strong Argentine presence the area was subjected to severe shelling from the Royal Navy.

The farm cemetery contains the grave of Captain Gavin John Hamilton MC of the Special Air Service who was killed while carrying out a reconnaissance exercise in the area.

A small museum next to the guest lodge is dedicated to the 1982 war.

Sheltered from the chilly south wind by majestic Mount Adam and overlooking Saunders Island, Hill Cove settlement nestles on the shore of Byron Sound on the north coast of West Falklands.

New Zealanders Wickham Bertrand, Ernest Holmested and John Switzer originally leased Hill Cove in 1868, although at this time the settlement was situated to the northeast at Shallow Bay and the entire farm known as Adelaide Station. Living conditions were tough with Holmested and Switzer, plus two farm hands, living in a 30ft by 10ft one storey house.

In 1872 the farm was divided into two parts; Bertrand retained the portion he named Roy Cove while Holmested adopted Shallow Bay. Switzer had returned to New Zealand on a charge of arson.

Robert Blake later joined Bertrand as a business partner in what was to become a highly successful sheep farm.

By 1882, now married and with families, the pair decided to run the station from separate bases. Bertrand remained at Shallow Bay while Blake moved to Hill Cove.

Hard work continued for many years and once the Holmesteds retired to England the farm continued to thrive under subsequent managers.

In 1886 Robert Blake took the brave step of planting an area of hawthorn trees; further tree plantings took place in 1925. The resulting Hill Cove 'forest' remains the largest in the Islands today.

In 1889 Sydney Miller joined the farm, first as assistant manager, then later on as manager.

He was followed in 1932 by Hugh Harding who was manager until 1953 when William Blake took over until 1965.

Blake was responsible for notable farm improvement, and for the first time in many years the farm bred enough replacement sheep that purchase of stock was unnecessary. Money was more plentiful at this time and new houses were built inside the settlement and outside.

William Blake was followed by his cousin Tim Blake who managed the farm until 1987 when Hill Cove was sold for subdivision into eight sections.

Hill Cove is made up of two main settlements 'top' and 'bottom'.

The official port of entry for West Falklands, Fox Bay Village (East) faces Fox Bay West across an exposed harbour positioned on the south east coast of West Falklands.

Captain John Byron named the Bay when he surveyed the area in 1765 and observed large numbers of the Warrah 'fox' (Dusciyon australis).

The Packe brothers first leased Fox Bay East in the 1860s and Messrs Ballion and Stickney founded Fox Bay West around the same time. After purchase by the Falkland Islands Company the latter farm became the main settlement.

Originally the farm was stocked with Lincoln sheep but later it became one of the pioneer breeders of the Polwarth sheep which has since become one of the favoured breeds in Falklands' flocks today.

The east settlement was once the residence of the West Falklands doctor, postmaster, policeman (whose house contained a jail) and a wireless station.

In the early 1980s the farms were divided into sections and sold to residents. The Falkland Islands Government retained Fox Bay East settlement in order to continue its role as a government centre on West Falklands.

During the Falklands War Fox Bay was occupied by around 800 Argentine troops. Resident Nigel Knight describes an incident during the occupation, "Probably the most worrying was when I 'acquired' some secret Argentine codes which I had photographed for the British. I returned them before they were missed and I had just taken the film out of the camera when the Argentines carried out one of their random house searches..".

Fox Bay was strafed by British aircraft and bombarded by the Royal Navy on a number of occasions.

One year after the War it was renamed Fox Bay Village to illustrate its community function. After adoption as a village a wool mill was established, however, it did not prove to be viable due to the cost of energy.

Fox Bay East was the home of the artist Richard Cockwell who managed the farm from 1969. Richard's son Ben and his wife Clare reside at Fox Bay Village.

PORT EDGAR
26-1-09

Boasting a wonderfully large sheltered harbour, Port Edgar, situated on the south west coast of Falkland Sound, was named after Lieutenant Thomas Edgar of Lydd of the United Kingdom

Edgar who surveyed around the Falklands in 1786-87 on board the whaler *Hope*, also served as Master on the *Discovery* during Captain James Cook's third voyage to the Pacific (1776-1780).

Port Edgar farm, once double its current size, was originally leased and then owned by Mr C H Williams.

Williams, who was in debt to farming brothers, the Deans, sold the pair the section that included Dyke Island in 1874. (Williams continued to farm the Weddell Group).

Dean Brothers also owned neighbouring Port Stephens and the purchase of Port Edgar was a vital one.

At this time sheep were ravaged by 'scab' and with the act of buying Port Edgar the farm reduced its boundary to only one mile.

The addition of Port Edgar also meant Port Stephens farm totalled 250,000 acres, a thousand miles of coastline and 27,254 sheep.

The grave of a 10 year old boy, Alfred Anderson can be found at Port Edgar. Alfred's father is likely to have been a manager at Port Edgar in the 1890s.

In the 1940s Dean Brothers sold the farm to the Falkland Islands Company with whom it stayed until 1988 when it was purchased as a smaller section by Tex and Mandy Alazia.

Port Edgar is now approximately 39,536 acres and boasts 6,100 Corriedale sheep.

The farm was certified organic in 1998 with the Falkland Islands Development Corporation and later with the Biological Farmers of Australia.

The owners sell their finer wool as organic but they also view being 'green and clean' as a way of life.

The Alazias harness wind power, work their sheep flocks on foot and use sheep dogs.

Port Edgar is a largely self sufficient farm and the owners believe in the best possible animal husbandry.

Sea Lion Island, although at one stage in its history unable to entirely escape the clutches of sealers and penguin hunters, has primarily functioned as a sheep farm.

In 1892 the British vessel *Viscount* fell victim to seas around the Falklands and the debris was used to build the farmhouse on the island.

Situated to the south of East Falklands the island was first farmed by the Ricketts family, but the isolation brought with it a number of difficulties. Once when a farm worker fell ill help was sought from the mainland, and one brave soul rowed to the island in a raft made from a barrel.

There is no harbour on the steep sided but fairly flat island thus provisions are hoisted up a ramp by block and tackle from a natural stone landing stage at the bottom of a deep gulch.

The arrival of the DeHavilland Beaver float plane in the Falkland Islands in 1953, relieved communications to some degree, however, when visiting, the pilot had no alternative but to land on a shallow pond at the west end of the island. With the advent of wheeled planes in the Falklands an airstrip was built.

After several owners the island was sold and a lodge built where visitors could stay in comfort while enjoying the wildlife. Sea Lion Lodge was operated by the Gray family.

Since 1995, a team of Italian researchers have been conducting a long-term study of the southern elephant seals of Sea Lion Island.

Today the island is owned by the Falkland Islands Development Corporation and is run solely as a wildlife haven and is a popular visitor destination.

Over the years sheep numbers were gradually reduced to nothing; as a result the grasses have thrived providing excellent cover for small birds including the endemic Cobb's wren.

The island is famous for offering regular sightings of Killer whale pods close to the eastern beaches.

On Bull Hill in the south of the island there is a memorial to the British warship HMS *Sheffield* sunk in 1982.

The Island is 2,236 acres (905 ha.)

West of West Falklands and north of Beaver Island sits the beautiful wildlife haven, New Island.

Referred to as 'New Isle' in one of the earliest log books cited, it is a reference by the early whalers to their discoveries of island groups and whaling grounds. Whalers from Nantucket entered the harbours of New Island between 1772 and 1774.

The master of one of the early whalers that anchored at New Island nearly 200 years ago wrote "The scenery is altogether sublime beyond description. Viewed many of the wonders of nature in the perpendicular cliffs which bound the seaboard sides of this island."

It is a description fitting the island's landscape today.

New Island is one of a number of islands forming a small archipelago.

Islands such as Pitt, Barclay, Quaker, Fox, Coffin, Beaver and Penn, bear names closely associated with Nantucket whalers and the Quaker families who operated the whale oil business and owned the majority of the Nantucket whaling ships.

New Island was to become an important base and self styled home for the whalers and so commenced a long and often complex history of exploitation of the island's natural wealth.

The island's huge penguin and albatross colonies provided food in the form of eggs and its geese were a source of fresh meat.

For over 200 years New Island was to see a succession of industries aimed at exploiting its natural wealth. Whales were hunted within the headlands of the island, sealing, penguin oiling and a guano industry attempted.

Some time between 1851 and 1860 the island saw the commencement of sheep and cattle farming with the first official settlement of the island. The stocking and settlement of New Island, with a succession of leases and owners was then to continue virtually without a break until 1972.

In 1972 New Island experienced a change in its long history of exploitation when it was purchased with the sole aim of establishing it as a wildlife reserve. Under the Trust it will remain a wildlife reserve in perpetuity.

New Island is 5,840 acres (2,363 ha).

Named after First Lord of the Admiralty, Admiral Augustus Keppel, the island of Keppel is an important one in Falklands history

Situated off the north coast of West Falklands, Keppel Island was chosen by Captain Parker Snow in the schooner *Allen Gardiner* as a suitable island in the Falklands on which the South American Missionary Society (SAMS) could establish a mission for the education, 'civilization' and Christian conversion of the Southern Patagonian (Fuegian) Yaghan Indians.

The first of these were encouraged to travel to Keppel around 1858. During its lifetime well over 150 Fuegians were brought to the settlement.

Over the next two years the missionaries laboured to establish the settlement naming it Cranmer Station after the Protestant martyr.

The mission superintendent was installed in a wooden house on an elevated site, a store was built, gardens were dug and planted.

The Mission was not without conflict and clashes of culture, and ultimately many of the Yaghans died of 'modern' diseases.

The Mission Society continued to function until 1898 when the Fuegians left, and the island was continued as a farm.

Names most associated with Keppel include Yaghan Jemmy Button, who was taken to London on the *Beagle* and entertained by the King and Queen, and Thomas Bridges who later produced a comprehensive dictionary of the Yaghan language.

Some Islanders today still have documentation showing ancestors christened by Thomas Bridges.

Keppel was eventually sold to Dean Brothers of Pebble, followed by the Miller family and then Mr Lionel Fell. Eventually the island proved uneconomical as a sheep farm and it stands unoccupied today, although the Mission buildings still remain as foundations or standing structures.

The present wool shed was the Mission's chapel and bears the original emblem over the door with the initials SAMS.

There is also a cemetery containing the graves and headstones of missionaries and Fuegian Indians.

Keppel is 8,960 acres (3,626 ha).

ℛ

FLINDERS ISLAND
(THE NECK)
1/3/09

It was on Saunders Island that Commodore John Byron claimed the Falkland Islands for Britain on January 25th, 1765, and founded Port Egmont, which he named after the First Lord of the Admiralty then, the politician, John Perceval, 2nd Earl of Egmont.

The island itself is named after Admiral Sir Charles Saunders KB who as a young man, like Byron himself, had accompanied Lord Anson on his famous voyage around the world in 1740-44.

In September 1765 British ships under the command of Captain John McBride set sail to establish a permanent settlement on the islands arriving at Port Egmont on January 8, 1766.

Unaware of the French Settlement at Port Louis, McBride set about creating a substantial shore settlement at Port Egmont.

In December of that year, McBride discovered Port Louis and informed the French commander of the Port Egmont colony. Both men reiterated their countries' claims to sovereignty.

The Spanish pressured the French into handing Port Louis over to them and on June 10, 1770, Spanish troops and vessels made a surprise attack on Port Egmont forcing the small British garrison to capitulate.

This brought Britain and Spain close to war. However, war was avoided by an agreement, dated January 22, 1771, by which Spain was forced to restore Port Egmont, which Britain re-occupied later that year, both sides maintaining their sovereignty claims to all the archipelago.

Britain withdrew the garrison from Port Egmont in 1774 during the reployment of British forces to face the approaching American War of Independence. A plaque was left restating the British claim to sovereignty over the Falkland Islands, although this was subsequently removed by the Spanish.

The port continued to be used intermittently by British and American sealers, and the Spanish made annual visits in an attempt to stop them. The Spanish authorities finally destroyed the settlement on instructions from Madrid, in 1780, by which time Spain was at war with Britain.

In 1987 the Pole-Evans family, long term managers of the farm, were able to purchase, and continue it as a sheep station and offer self catering to guests.

The island is 31,000 acres (12,545 ha).

Once a haven for eighteenth century sealers West Point Island is situated to the far northwest of West Falklands,

Formerly known as Albatross Island (due to the presence of many thousands of pairs) the sealers that adopted it as a base, used it to access water, take rest from voyages and even plant potatoes as a source of fresh vegetables.

The ships' crews also put the first cattle ashore to provide fresh meat.

Around 1820 the sloop *Penguin* was one of the primary seal hunting vessels on West Falklands.

Larger vessels would anchor in West Point Harbour in order to receive seal skins before the onward journey.

A sealers' trypot used for rendering down the fat of the mammal still remains on the island.

Originally part of Roy Cove Farm in 1879 Arthur Felton leased the island from his brother-in-law Bertrand, who owned Roy Cove.

When Felton took charge of the island, he and his brother occasionally invited naval personnel from visiting ships on horseback chases to assist in culling the cattle left by the sealers.

Felton initially lived in a tiny stone building erected by sealers, however, he later built more permanent accommodation and other farm buildings including the shearing shed.

Ahead of his time as a conservationist West Point was fortunate in having Arthur Felton as its manager. He was energetic in replanting many thousands of tussac plants and trees and in protecting the wildlife.

By 1910 Felton had replanted almost the entire northern coastline.

West Point continued as a small but thriving sheep farm under his management, and after he died it was purchased by his niece Gladys 'Muzzie' Napier.

Muzzie's son Roddy inherited the island and he and his wife Lily continued the tradition of conservation and currently share its many natural attractions with passengers from visiting small cruise ships.

West Point's history is prettily captured in such names as Felton's Rocks, Napier's Hill and Muzzie's Paddock.

West Point Island is 2,700 acres (1,255 ha).

Geographically distinct from the rest of the Falklands Islands the dramatic peaks of the Jason Islands may have been the first of the Falkland Islands sighted by early sailors of the South Atlantic.

Situated to the far north west of West Falklands the chain of islands was first recorded by Dutch navigator Sebald de Weert in 1600 during his homeward leg to the Netherlands. De Weert named them the Sebaldines.

In 1766 Captain John McBride during a naval survey of the Falklands renamed the islands for his ship HMS *Jason*.

Rich in wildlife the islands soon came to the notice of penguin hunters. In the 18th and 19th centuries millions of rockhopper and gentoo penguins were killed and boiled to extract their oil.

Evidence of the industry exists in the form of rusting trypots in bays, and countless penguin bones and skulls in the southern part of Steeple Jason at The Neck.

From 1872 for approximately 100 years sheep were grazed on the two larger islands but falling wool prices and the unpredictable weather conditions for local cutters made stocking sheep and transporting wool uneconomical. Two buildings still remain on the islands from this time.

In March 1970, the Jasons were purchased by Len Hill for £5,500. Len Hill once famously released banknotes in the Jason Islands name in order to raise money for conservation there. Signed by Len Hill the notes indicate validity until December 31, 1979.

In the 1990s Steeple Jason and Grand Jason were sold to New York philanthropist Michael Steinhardt who donated them to the Wildlife Conservation Society at the Bronx Zoo, New York. Steinhardt also provided funding to build a conservation station.

Today small cruise vessels pay visits to the islands when the difficult sea conditions allow landings.

The group includes Steeple Island, Grand Island, Elephant Island, Flat Island and South Island with Steeple and Grand being the largest.

The Jasons Island chain stretches for 40 miles with Grand and Steeple Jason rising to around 1,000 ft.

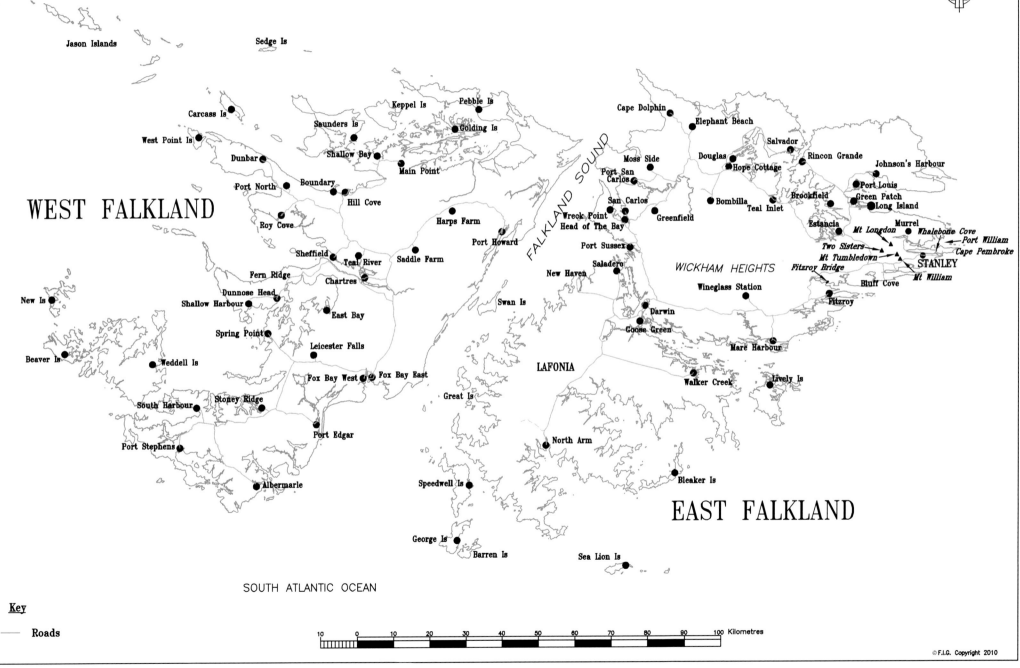

# FALKLAND ISLANDS

SOUTH ATLANTIC OCEAN

Jason Islands

Sedge Is

Carcass Is

West Point Is

Keppel Is

Pebble Is

Saunders Is

Golding Is

Shallow Bay

Dunbar

Main Point

Boundary

Port North

Hill Cove

**WEST FALKLAND**

Roy Cove

Harps Farm

Cape Dolphin

Elephant Beach

Moss Side

Salvador

Rincon Grande

Douglas

Johnson's Harbour

Port San Carlos

Hope Cottage

Brookfield

Port Louis

Bombilla

Teal Inlet

Green Patch

San Carlos

Long Island

Greenfield

Estancia

Murrel

Wreck Point

Head of The Bay

Mt Longdon

Whalebone Cove

Two Sisters

Port William

Sheffield

Teal River

Saddle Farm

Port Howard

Mt Tumbledown

Cape Pembroke

Port Sussex

STANLEY

Fern Ridge

Chartres

WICKHAM HEIGHTS

Fitzroy Bridge

Mt William

Dunnose Head

Saladero

New Haven

Bluff Cove

New Is

Shallow Harbour

East Bay

Swan Is

Wineglass Station

Fitzroy

Spring Point

Beaver Is

Weddell Is

Leicester Falls

Darwin

Mare Harbour

Goose Green

South Harbour

Stoney Ridge

LAFONIA

Fox Bay West

Fox Bay East

Great Is

Walker Creek

Lively Is

Port Edgar

Port Stephens

North Arm

**EAST FALKLAND**

Albermarle

Speedwell Is

Bleaker Is

George Is

Barren Is

Sea Lion Is

SOUTH ATLANTIC OCEAN

FALKLAND SOUND

## Key

— Roads

10  0  10  20  30  40  50  60  70  80  90  100 Kilometres